Alphabet Readers

Exploring Letter-Sound Relationships within Meaningful Content

by
Sherrill B. Flora

illustrated by
Vanessa Countryman

Publisher
Key Education Publishing Company, LLC
Minneapolis, Minnesota

CONTENTS

How To Use This Book

Alphabet Readers includes thirty-one reproducible storybooks consisting of twenty-one beginning consonant sound stories, five short vowel sound stories, and five long vowel sound stories. Word lists and additional alphabet activities are included on the last page of each storybook.

Directions: Reproduce a storybook for each child. Color, cut out along the dotted lines, and staple the pages in numerical order.

Follow all the reading suggestions and activities found on the last page of each storybook.

The children in your classroom will be thrilled when they are allowed to keep and bring home the storybooks that they have learned to read at school. What an easy and inexpensive way to get reading materials into the hands of children and their families. Watch the eyes of the children light up as they get to keep each new story!

Credits

Author: Sherrill B. Flora
Inside Illustrations: Vanessa Countryman
Creative Director: Mary Claire
Cover Design: Mary Eden
Editor: George C. Flora

Key Education welcomes manuscripts and product ideas from teachers. For a copy of our submission guidelines, please send a self-addressed, stamped envelope to:

Key Education Publishing Company, LLC.
Acquisitions Department
9601 Newton Avenue South
Minneapolis, Minnesota 55431

ISBN: 1-933052-04-X
Alphabet Readers
Copyright © 2005 by Key Education Publishing Company, LLC
Minneapolis, Minnesota 55431

2

Little ant had a map.

4

He ran and ran and ran.

(Short Sound) Letter "Aa" Story

Ant and the Map

1

3

Ant had to follow the path.

6

Ant had to go back to the path.

5

Ant sat down. Can he last?

7

Look! Many ants are eating apples.

8

Notes to Teachers/Parents

DIRECTIONS TO MAKE THE BOOK: Copy the storybook for each student. Color and cut out along the dotted lines. Staple the eight pages together in numerical order.

BEFORE READING

1. Read the list of short "**Aa**" words that appear in the story: **ant, ants, and, back, apples, had, can, path, map, ran, last, sat.**

2. Discuss the other words in the story: **little, to, down, eating, the, follow, look, a, he, go, are.**

3. Have the children look at the text and circle each uppercase **A** and lowercase **a**.

AFTER READING

1. Together read and discuss the story.

2. There are more pictures in the story that have the short "**Aa**" sound. Can you find them? *(cap, bag, basket)*

MORE SHORT "Aa" ACTIVITIES

1. Make your own map.

2. Make a thumbprint ant.

3. Search for letter **Aa** in old newspapers. Cut them out.

2

Ray and May are Blue Jays.

4

They love to bake cakes.

(Long Sound) Letter "Aa" Story

Ray and May
Blue Jay

1

3

They play all day.

6

They love to paint on paper.

8

Notes to Teachers/Parents

DIRECTIONS TO MAKE THE BOOK: Copy the storybook for each student. Color and cut out along the dotted lines. Staple the eight pages together in numerical order.

BEFORE READING ---------------
1. Read the list of long "**Aa**" words that appear in the story: **Ray, May, jay, jays, bake, cakes, play, paper, paint, day, make, a, games.**
2. Discuss the other words in the story: **are, blue, all, they, love, to, and, on, fun.**
3. Have the children look at the text and circle each lowercase **a**.

AFTER READING ---------------
1. Together read and discuss the story.
2. There are more pictures in the story that have the long "**Aa**" sound. Can you find them? *(apron, frame, plate, roller blades or skates)*

MORE LONG "Aa" ACTIVITIES ---------------
1. Decorate a paper plate.
2. Make new words with these word families: –ay, –ate, and –ake.

5

They love to play games.

7

Ray and May
make fun all day.

Letter "Bb" Story

Bobby Bear's Big Day

Today is Bobby Bear's big day.

Bobby Bear got his bag.

Bobby Bear got his ball.

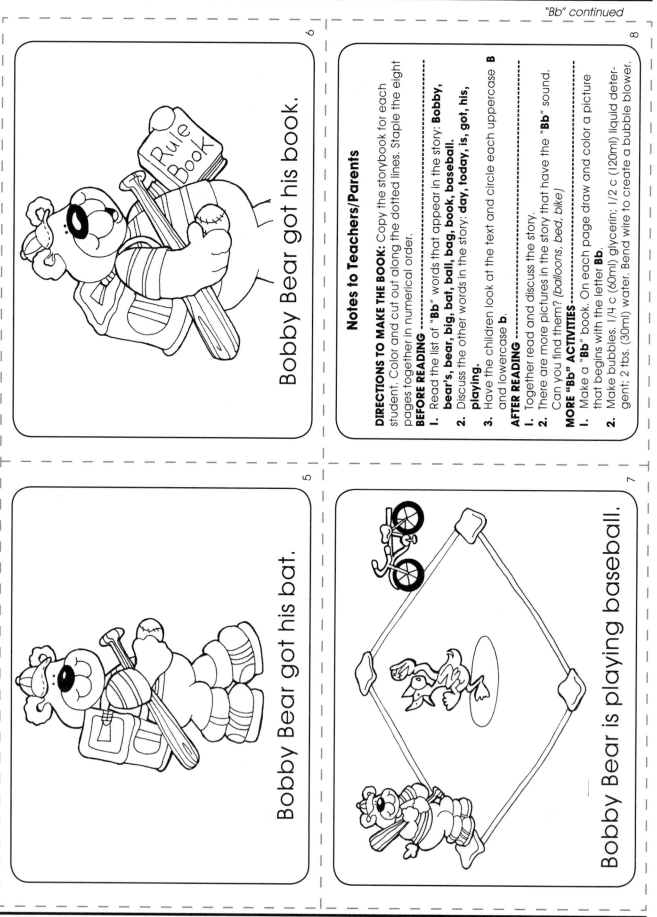

6

Bobby Bear got his book.

8

Notes to Teachers/Parents

DIRECTIONS TO MAKE THE BOOK: Copy the storybook for each student. Color and cut out along the dotted lines. Staple the eight pages together in numerical order.

BEFORE READING
1. Read the list of **"Bb"** words that appear in the story: **Bobby, bear's, bear, big, bat, ball, bag, book, baseball.**
2. Discuss the other words in the story: **day, today, is, got, his, playing.**
3. Have the children look at the text and circle each uppercase **B** and lowercase **b**.

AFTER READING
1. Together read and discuss the story.
2. There are more pictures in the story that have the **"Bb"** sound. Can you find them? *(balloons, bed, bike)*

MORE "Bb" ACTIVITIES
1. Make a **"Bb"** book. On each page draw and color a picture that begins with the letter **Bb**.
2. Make bubbles. 1/4 c (60ml) glycerin; 1/2 c (120ml) liquid detergent; 2 tbs. (30ml) water. Bend wire to create a bubble blower.

5

Bobby Bear got his bat.

7

Bobby Bear is playing baseball.

Letter "Cc" Story

Carly Cow Can

Carly Cow can cook.
Can you?

Carly Cow can cut.
Can you?

Carly Cow can clean.
Can you?

6

Carly Cow can drive a car. Can you?

8

Notes to Teachers/Parents

DIRECTIONS TO MAKE THE BOOK: Copy the storybook for each student. Color and cut out along the dotted lines. Staple the eight pages together in numerical order.

BEFORE READING ⎯⎯⎯⎯⎯⎯⎯⎯⎯⎯⎯⎯⎯⎯
1. Read the list of "**Cc**" words that appear in the story: **Carly, cow, can, cook, clean, cut, count, car, corn.**
2. Discuss the other words in the story: **you, drive, eat, a.**
3. Have the children look at the text and circle each uppercase **C** and lowercase **c**.

AFTER READING ⎯⎯⎯⎯⎯⎯⎯⎯⎯⎯⎯⎯⎯⎯⎯
1. Together read and discuss the story.
2. There are more pictures in the story that have the "**Cc**" sound. Can you find them? *(cat, coat, cookies, candle)*

MORE "Cc" ACTIVITIES ⎯⎯⎯⎯⎯⎯⎯⎯⎯⎯⎯
1. Bake chocolate chip cookies.
2. Draw a cake. Then draw candles on the cake.
3. Decorate a juice can and use it for storing color crayons.

5

Carly Cow can count. Can you?

7

Carly Cow can eat corn. Can you?

Letter "Dd" Story

What is dog doing?

1

Did you see
the dog digging?

2

Yes, I did.
What is he doing?

3

Did you see
the dog digging?

4

6

Did you see
the dog digging?

8

Notes to Teachers/Parents

DIRECTIONS TO MAKE THE BOOK: Copy the storybook for each student. Color and cut out along the dotted lines. Staple the eight pages together in numerical order.

BEFORE READING

1. Read the list of "**Dd**" words that appear in the story: **dig, dog, doing, digging, dinosaur, did.**
2. Discuss the other words in the story: **you, see, what, is, yes, I, he, up, a, bone, the.**
3. Have the children look at the text and circle each uppercase **D** and lowercase **d.**

AFTER READING

1. Together read and discuss the story.
2. There are more pictures in the story that have the "**Dd**" sound. Can you find them? (deer, duck, donut)

MORE "Dd" ACTIVITIES

1. Play a game of dominoes.
2. Look through magazines and cut out pictures of dogs.
3. Use clay or playdough and make a dinosaur.

5

Yes, I did.
What is he doing?

7

Yes, I did! Dog is digging
up a dinosaur bone!

(Short Sound) Letter "Ee" Story

Let's Help Hen

1

Let's help hen build a nest.

2

Elephant can help.

3

Elf can help.

4

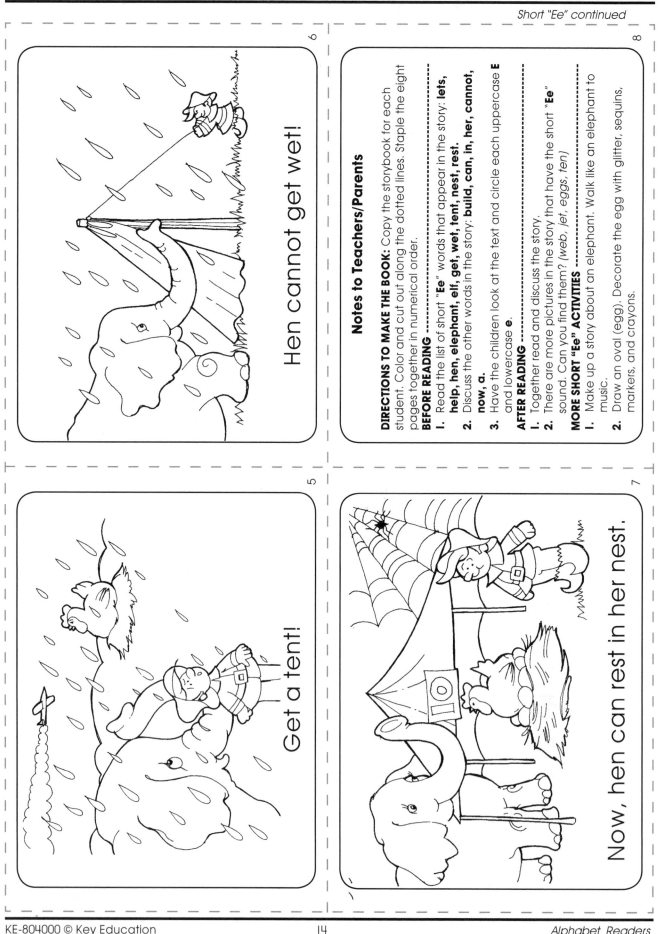

6

Hen cannot get wet!

8

Notes to Teachers/Parents

DIRECTIONS TO MAKE THE BOOK: Copy the storybook for each student. Color and cut out along the dotted lines. Staple the eight pages together in numerical order.

BEFORE READING

1. Read the list of short **"Ee"** words that appear in the story: **lets, help, hen, elephant, elf, get, wet, tent, nest, rest.**
2. Discuss the other words in the story: **build, can, in, her, cannot, now, a.**
3. Have the children look at the text and circle each uppercase **E** and lowercase **e.**

AFTER READING

1. Together read and discuss the story.
2. There are more pictures in the story that have the short **"Ee"** sound. Can you find them? *(web, jet, eggs, ten)*

MORE SHORT "Ee" ACTIVITIES

1. Make up a story about an elephant. Walk like an elephant to music.
2. Draw an oval (egg). Decorate the egg with glitter, sequins, markers, and crayons.

5

Get a tent!

7

Now, hen can rest in her nest.

2

Three bees play hide and seek.

4

The bees peek by the tree.

(Long Sound) Letter "Ee" Story

Can You See Me?

1

3

Can you see me?

6

The bees peek by the jeep.

5

Can you see me?

Notes to Teachers/Parents

DIRECTIONS TO MAKE THE BOOK: Copy the storybook for each student. Color and cut out along the dotted lines. Staple the eight pages together in numerical order.

BEFORE READING
1. Read the list of long **"Ee"** words that appear in the story: **three, bee, bees, me, jeep, see, peek, sleeping, tree.**
2. Discuss the other words in the story: **you, can, play, hide, and, the by, is.**
3. Have the children look at the text and circle each lowercase **e.**

AFTER READING
1. Together read and discuss the story.
2. There are more pictures in the story that have the long **"Ee"** sound. Can you find them? *(leaf)*

MORE LONG "Ee" ACTIVITIES
1. Learn the rhyme, *Eency, Weency, Spider.*
2. How many words can you make using the following word families: –ee, –eek, –eep?
3. Using green playdough, mold an **"E"** and an **"e."**

8

7

See! Bee is sleeping.

2

Fox is fishing.

4

The fish fooled me!
It is a feather!

Letter "Ff" Story

Fox is fishing!

1

3

The fish fooled me!
It is a fan!

6

I will get that fish!

5

The fish fooled me!
It is a football.

8

Notes to Teachers/Parents

DIRECTIONS TO MAKE THE BOOK: Copy the storybook for each student. Color and cut out along the dotted lines. Staple the eight pages together in numerical order.

BEFORE READING
1. Read the list of "**Ff**" words that appear in the story: **fox, fish, fishing, fooled, fan, feather, football, fell.**
2. Discuss the other words in the story: **is, me, the, again, it, a, I, water, that, will, get, in.**
3. Have the children look at the text and circle each uppercase **F** and lowercase **f**.

AFTER READING
1. Together read and discuss the story.
2. There are more pictures in the story that have the "**Ff**" sound. Can you find them? *(falling, fire, fork)*

MORE "Ff" ACTIVITIES
1. Trace and color a drawing of your feet.
2. Sing, *Five Green and Speckled Frogs.*
3. Make a fishing game. Cut out fish from card stock and add a paper clip. Use a yardstick with string and a magnet attached as the fishing rod.

7

Fooled again!
Fox fell in the water!

Letter "Gg" Story

Goat and Gorilla Giggle

Goat and gorilla were good friends.

Go fish!

They giggled playing games.

Everything they did made them giggle.

6

They giggled giving gifts.

5

They giggled in the garden.

Notes to Teachers/Parents

DIRECTIONS TO MAKE THE BOOK: Copy the storybook for each student. Color and cut out along the dotted lines. Staple the eight pages together in numerical order.

BEFORE READING

1. Read the list of "**Gg**" words that appear in the story: **goat, gorilla, good, giggled, games, garden, giving, gifts, giggly.**

2. Discuss the other words in the story: **and, were, friends, everything, they, did, made, them, playing, in, the**

3. Have the children look at the text and circle each uppercase **G** and lowercase **g**.

AFTER READING

1. Together read and discuss the story.

2. There are more pictures in the story that have the "**Gg**" sound. Can you find them? ("Go fish," guitar, gate)

MORE "Gg" ACTIVITIES

1. Read Goldilocks and the Three Bears and The Three Billy Goats Gruff. Listen for the "**Gg**" sound.

2. Make a gumdrop tree. Put clay in the bottom of a cup. Place a small branch in the clay. Put a gumdrop on the end of each branch.

8

7

They were giggly good friends.

2

Hilda Horse said,
"How do I look?"

4

Hilda Horse said,
"How do I look?"

Letter "Hh" Story

Hilda's Horrible Hat

1

3

"It is a horrible hat,"
said Henry.

6

Hilda Horse said,
"How do I look?"

8

Notes to Teachers/Parents

DIRECTIONS TO MAKE THE BOOK: Copy the storybook for each student. Color and cut out along the dotted lines. Staple the eight pages together in numerical order.

BEFORE READING
1. Read the list of "**Hh**" words that appear in the story: **how, Hilda, horse, Henry, horrible, hat, hooray.**
2. Discuss the other words in the story: **do, I, look, said, it, is, a, that, good, to, eat.**
3. Have the children look at the text and circle each uppercase **H** and lowercase **h**.

AFTER READING
1. Together read and discuss the story.
2. There are more pictures in the story that have the "**Hh**" sound. Can you find them? *(house, heart, hen)*

MORE "Hh" ACTIVITIES
1. Draw and color a new hat for Hilda.
2. Draw a hopscotch grid. Draw pictures that begin with the "Hh" sound in each box.
3. Learn the nursery rhyme, *Humpty Dumpty.*

5

"It is a horrible hat,"
said Henry.

7

"Hooray! A hat that is
good to eat," said Henry.

(Short Sound) Letter "Ii" Story

Little Baby Pig

This is little baby pig.

Little baby pig is in his crib.

Little baby pig wears a bib.

2

1

3

4

23

6

Little baby pig dances a jig.

5

Little baby pig wears a wig.

8

Notes to Teachers/Parents

DIRECTIONS TO MAKE THE BOOK: Copy the storybook for each student. Color and cut out along the dotted lines. Staple the eight pages together in numerical order.

BEFORE READING
1. Read the list of short "Ii" words that appear in the story: **this, little, pig, is, crib, bib, wig, jig, in, his, silly.**
2. Discuss the other words in the story: **baby, wears, a, dances.**
3. Have the children look at the text and circle each lowercase **i.**

AFTER READING
1. Together read and discuss the story.
2. There are more pictures in the story that have the short "Ii" sound. Can you find them? *(fish, dish)*

MORE SHORT "Ii" ACTIVITIES
1. Learn the rhyme, *Itsy, Bitsy Spider.*
2. Draw an inchworm.
3. Make an igloo by gluing sugar cubes together.
4. How many words can you make using the following word families: –it, –in, –ig, –Ill?

7

Silly little baby pig.

2

Five mice like to ride bikes.

4

Five mice like to glide.

(Long Sound) Letter "Ii" Story

Five Mice

1

3

Five mice like to hike.

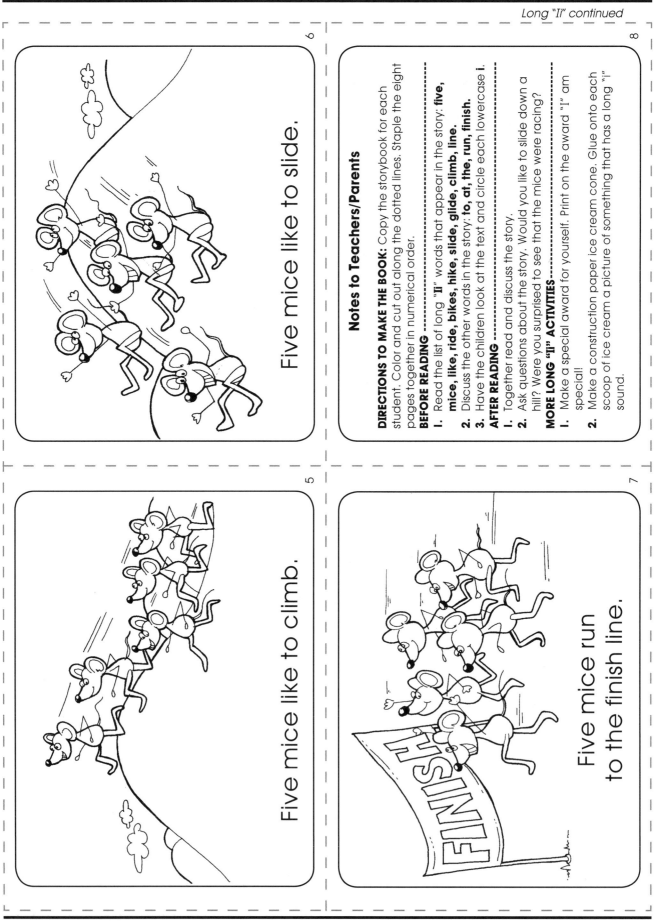

6

Five mice like to slide.

5

Five mice like to climb.

Notes to Teachers/Parents

DIRECTIONS TO MAKE THE BOOK: Copy the storybook for each student. Color and cut out along the dotted lines. Staple the eight pages together in numerical order.

BEFORE READING ─────────────────────

1. Read the list of long "Ii" words that appear in the story: **five, mice, like, ride, bikes, hike, slide, glide, climb, line.**
2. Discuss the other words in the story: **to, at, the, run, finish.**
3. Have the children look at the text and circle each lowercase **i.**

AFTER READING ─────────────────────

1. Together read and discuss the story.
2. Ask questions about the story. Would you like to slide down a hill? Were you surprised to see that the mice were racing?

MORE LONG "Ii" ACTIVITIES ───────────

1. Make a special award for yourself. Print on the award "I" am special!
2. Make a construction paper ice cream cone. Glue onto each scoop of ice cream a picture of something that has a long "I" sound.

8

7

Five mice run
to the finish line.

Letter "Jj" Story

Who Can Jump?

1

Can a jeep jump? No!

2

Can jam and jelly jump? No!

3

Can jacks jump? No!

4

6

Can Joe and the jack-in-the box jump? No!

8

Notes to Teachers/Parents

DIRECTIONS TO MAKE THE BOOK: Copy the storybook for each student. Color and cut out along the dotted lines. Staple the eight pages together in numerical order.

BEFORE READING
1. Read the list of "Jj" words that appear in the story: **jump, jeep, jet, jam, jacks, Joe, jelly, jack.**
2. Discuss the other words in the story: **yes, they, can, a, no, in, the, box, and.**
3. Have the children look at the text and circle each uppercase **J** and lowercase **j**.

AFTER READING
1. Together read and discuss the story.

MORE "Jj" ACTIVITIES
1. Make gelatin jigglers. Use 2 1/2 cups of boiling water or apple juice, and add two 8 ounce packages of flavored gelatin. Mix together for at least 3 minutes. Pour into a 9" x 13" pan and refrigerate for at least 3 hours. Cut out shapes with cookie cutters.
2. Sing, *Jack and Jill* and *John Jacob Jingleheimer Schmidt.*

5

Can a jet jump? No!

7

Yes, they can!

2

Katie Kitten
went to see the king.

4

Katie and the king
flew the kite.

Letter "Kk" Story

1

**Katie
Kitten
and the
King**

3

Katie gave the king a kite.

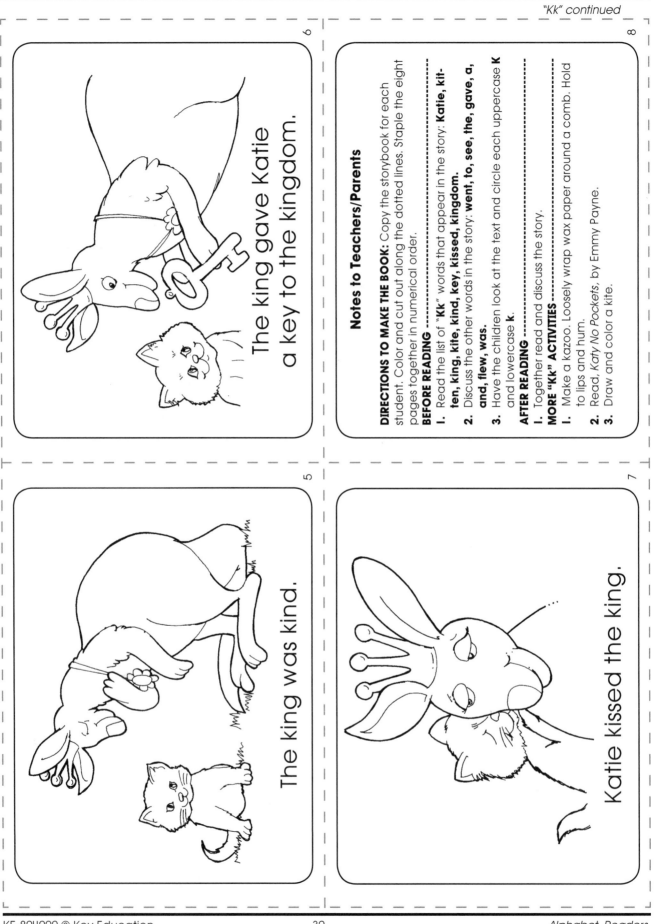

6

The king gave Katie a key to the kingdom.

5

The king was kind.

7

Katie kissed the king.

8

Notes to Teachers/Parents

DIRECTIONS TO MAKE THE BOOK: Copy the storybook for each student. Color and cut out along the dotted lines. Staple the eight pages together in numerical order.

BEFORE READING

1. Read the list of **"Kk"** words that appear in the story: **Katie, kitten, king, kite, kind, key, kissed, kingdom.**

2. Discuss the other words in the story: **went, to, see, the, gave, a, and, flew, was.**

3. Have the children look at the text and circle each uppercase **K** and lowercase **k.**

AFTER READING

1. Together read and discuss the story.

MORE "Kk" ACTIVITIES

1. Make a kazoo. Loosely wrap wax paper around a comb. Hold to lips and hum.

2. Read, *Katy No Pockets*, by Emmy Payne.

3. Draw and color a kite.

2

Look at little lion.

4

Look at little lemur.

Letter "Ll" Story

Look at the Little Friends

1

3

Look at little lamb.

6

Let's build.

8

Notes to Teachers/Parents

DIRECTIONS TO MAKE THE BOOK: Copy the storybook for each student. Color and cut out along the dotted lines. Staple the eight pages together in numerical order.

BEFORE READING

1. Read the list of "**Ll**" words that appear in the story: **look, little, lion, lemur, let's, large, lemonade.**

2. Discuss the other words in the story: **at, the, friends, box, build, a, stand.**

3. Have the children look at the text and circle each uppercase **L** and lowercase **l**.

AFTER READING

1. Together read and discuss the story.

2. There are more pictures in the story that have the "**Ll**" sound. Can you find them? *(ladder, lamp, lollipop)*

MORE "Ll" ACTIVITIES

1. Provide the child with an outline of a lamb. Brush diluted glue on the inside of the outline and fill with cotton.

2. Sing, *London Bridge* and *Loopy Loo.*

3. Play leap frog.

5

Look at the large box.

7

Look! A lemonade stand.

Lemonade

2

Mouse and monkey want to move to the moon.

4

They made a map.

Letter "Mm" Story

Mouse and Monkey

1

3

They want to see the man in the moon.

6

They see the man in the moon!

8

Notes to Teachers/Parents

DIRECTIONS TO MAKE THE BOOK: Copy the storybook for each student. Color and cut out along the dotted lines. Staple the eight pages together in numerical order.

BEFORE READING
1. Read the list of **"Mm"** words that appear in the story: **mouse, monkey, man, move, moon, make, map, masks.**
2. Discuss the other words in the story: **they, to, want, the, see, a, in, where, is, did, he, put, on.**
3. Have the children look at the text and circle each uppercase **M** and lowercase **m.**

AFTER READING
1. Together read and discuss the story.
2. There are more pictures in the story that have the **"Mm"** sound. Can you find them? *(milk, mop, mushroom)*

MORE "Mm" ACTIVITIES
1. Paint with marbles. Place a piece of paper in a 9" x 13" pan. With a spoon, dip the marbles in paint. Place the wet marbles in the pan and roll over the paper.
2. Sing, *The Mickey Mouse Song,* and march to the music.
3. Glue macaroni on the inside of a large uppercase **M.**

5

They put on moon masks.

7

Where is the man in the moon? Did he move?

Letter "Nn" Story

**No, No, No!
It's Not Time!**

"Is it time?" asked Ned.

"No! No! No!
Not yet!" said Nellie.

"Is it time?" asked Ned.

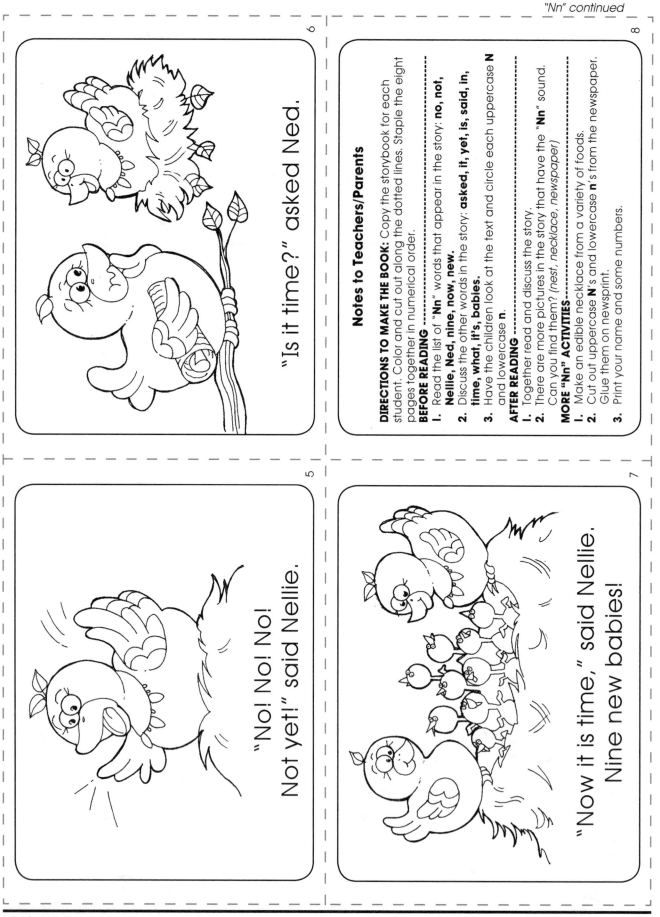

6

"Is it time?" asked Ned.

Notes to Teachers/Parents

DIRECTIONS TO MAKE THE BOOK: Copy the storybook for each student. Color and cut out along the dotted lines. Staple the eight pages together in numerical order.

BEFORE READING
1. Read the list of **"Nn"** words that appear in the story: **no, not, Nellie, Ned, nine, now, new.**
2. Discuss the other words in the story: **asked, it, yet, is, said, in, time, what, it's, babies.**
3. Have the children look at the text and circle each uppercase **N** and lowercase **n**.

AFTER READING
1. Together read and discuss the story.
2. There are more pictures in the story that have the **"Nn"** sound. Can you find them? *(nest, necklace, newspaper)*

MORE "Nn" ACTIVITIES
1. Make an edible necklace from a variety of foods.
2. Cut out uppercase **N**'s and lowercase **n**'s from the newspaper. Glue them on newsprint.
3. Print your name and some numbers.

5

"No! No! No!
Not yet!" said Nellie.

7

"Now it is time," said Nellie.
Nine new babies!

2

Fox lost his sock.

4

Is it in the box?

(Short Sound) Letter "Oo" Story

A Lost Sock

1

3

Is it in the pot?

6

Is it by the log?

8

Notes to Teachers/Parents

DIRECTIONS TO MAKE THE BOOK: Copy the storybook for each student. Color and cut out along the dotted lines. Staple the eight pages together in numerical order.

BEFORE READING
1. Read the list of short "Oo" words that appear in the story: **fox, lost, sock, pot, pond, log, stop, frog, box.**
2. Discuss the other words in the story: **his, is, it, in, the, by, that, my, a.**
3. Have the children look at the text and circle each lowercase **o.**

AFTER READING
1. Together read and discuss the story.
2. There is one more picture in the story that has the short "**Oo**" sound. Can you find it? (oven)

MORE SHORT "Oo" ACTIVITIES
1. Draw an octagon and print the word "stop."
2. Make some new words using these word families: –ot, –og, –ox. How many words can you make?
3. Draw and color a pizza with olives and onions.

5

Is it in the pond?

7

Stop frog!
That is my sock.

(Long Sound) Letter "Oo" Story

Oh No! Joe's Bone

1

Joe lost his bone.

2

Use your nose!

3

The bone is not by the soap.

4

6

The bone is not by the rose.

5

The bone is not by the boat.

8

Notes to Teachers/Parents

DIRECTIONS TO MAKE THE BOOK: Copy the storybook for each student. Color and cut out along the dotted lines. Staple the eight pages together in numerical order.

BEFORE READING
1. Read the list of long "Oo" words that appear in the story: **oh, no, Joe, bone, nose, soap, boat, rose, cone.**
2. Discuss the other words in the story: **his, use, your, the, is, not, by, in.**
3. Have the children look at the text and circle each uppercase **O** and lowercase **o**.

AFTER READING
1. Together read and discuss the story.

MORE LONG "Oo" ACTIVITIES
1. Draw an ocean and add some interesting fish.
2. Draw an oval. Brush the inside of the oval with diluted glue. Place cereal on the glue to make a mosaic.
3. Make some oatmeal.

7

The bone is in the cone.

2

Pass the peas, please.

4

Pass the potatoes, please.

1

Letter "Pp" Story

Porky Little Pigs

3

Pass the pancakes, please.

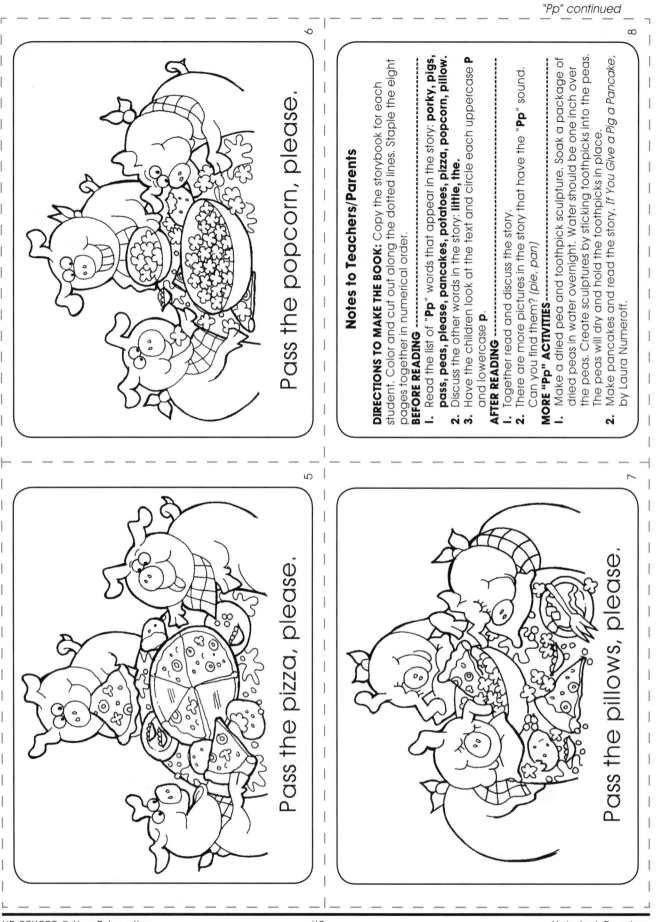

6

Pass the popcorn, please.

Notes to Teachers/Parents

DIRECTIONS TO MAKE THE BOOK: Copy the storybook for each student. Color and cut out along the dotted lines. Staple the eight pages together in numerical order.

BEFORE READING

1. Read the list of **"Pp"** words that appear in the story: **porky, pigs, pass, peas, please, pancakes, potatoes, pizza, popcorn, pillow.**
2. Discuss the other words in the story: **little, the.**
3. Have the children look at the text and circle each uppercase **P** and lowercase **p.**

AFTER READING

1. Together read and discuss the story.
2. There are more pictures in the story that have the **"Pp"** sound. Can you find them? *(pie, pan)*

MORE "Pp" ACTIVITIES

1. Make a dried pea and toothpick sculpture. Soak a package of dried peas in water overnight. Water should be one inch over the peas. Create sculptures by sticking toothpicks into the peas. The peas will dry and hold the toothpicks in place.
2. Make pancakes and read the story, *If You Give a Pig a Pancake,* by Laura Numeroff.

8

5

Pass the pizza, please.

Pass the pillows, please.

7

Letter "Qq" Story

Quack, Quack!

2

Under the quilt!
Did you hear a quack?

4

No, I think it was quiet.

1

3

The queen
questioned the maid.

6

The maid said, "It is quiet!"

Notes to Teachers/Parents

DIRECTIONS TO MAKE THE BOOK: Copy the storybook for each student. Color and cut out along the dotted lines. Staple the eight pages together in numerical order.

BEFORE READING

1. Read the list of "**Qq**" words that appear in the story: **quack, quilt, queen, questioned, quiet.**

2. Discuss the other words in the story: **I, heard, a, under, the, did, it's, you, hear, maid, no, it, was, said, is, duck, baby, think.**

3. Have the children look at the text and circle each uppercase **Q** and lowercase **q**.

AFTER READING

1. Together read and discuss the story.

MORE "Qq" ACTIVITIES

1. Paint with watercolors. Use Q-tips as a brush.

2. Play the game, *Quick, be Quiet!* Clap, sing, talk, and as soon as the leader says, "quick, be quiet," everyone must be quiet.

3. Make a quilt by gluing scraps of fabric on a piece of paper.

8

5

Under the quilt!
Did you hear a quack?

A quack from under the quilt.
Quiet, a baby duck!

7

2

Rabbit is ready
to run the race.

4

Raccoon is ready
to run the race.

1

Letter "Rr" Story

Rabbit Runs
the Race

3

Ready, set, run!

6

Robin is ready
to run the race.

8

Notes to Teachers/Parents

DIRECTIONS TO MAKE THE BOOK: Copy the storybook for each student. Color and cut out along the dotted lines. Staple the eight pages together in numerical order.

BEFORE READING
1. Read the list of **"Rr"** words that appear in the story: **rabbit, run, runs, race, ready, raccoon, robin, round.**
2. Discuss the other words in the story: **is, to, the, set, and, they.**
3. Have the children look at the text and circle each uppercase **R** and lowercase **r.**

AFTER READING
1. Together read and discuss the story.
2. There are more pictures in the story that have the **"Rr"** sound. Can you find them? *(rain, rake)*

MORE "Rr" ACTIVITIES
1. Sing, *Row, Row, Row Your Boat,* and *I've Been Working on the Railroad.*
2. Make a rock garden. Place 4 to 5 small damp sponges in the bottom of a tin pie pan. Sprinkle the following over the sponges: 4 tbs (60 ml) bluing; 4 tablespoons (60 ml) salt; and 1 tablespoon (15 ml) ammonia. The garden will begin growing within a few hours.

5

Ready, set, run!

7

Round and round they run!

FINISH

2

Six silly seals
sat in the sun.

4

Some sailed on the sea.

Letter "Ss" Story

Six Silly Seals

3

Six silly seals said,
"Let's have fun."

6

Some sat and sang.

8

Notes to Teachers/Parents

DIRECTIONS TO MAKE THE BOOK: Copy the storybook for each student. Color and cut out along the dotted lines. Staple the eight pages together in numerical order.

BEFORE READING --
1. Read the list of **"Ss"** words that appear in the story: **six, seals, sat, sun, said, some, sand, sailed, sea, sang.**
2. Discuss the other words in the story: **in, the, let's, have, fun, played, and, band, on.**
3. Have the children look at the text and circle each uppercase **S** and lowercase **s.**

AFTER READING --
1. Together read and discuss the story.
2. There are more pictures in the story that have the **"Ss"** sound. Can you find them? *(sunglasses, sailboat)*

MORE "Ss" ACTIVITIES --
1. Pretend you are spies. Attach a string to two juice cans and listen to the sounds.
2. Make playdough snakes that are shaped like an **"S."**

5

Some played in the sand.

7

Some played in the band.

Alphabet Readers

2

Two turtles at play.

4

They play with a top.

Two Turtles

1

3

They have tons of toys.

6

They watch TV.

8

Notes to Teachers/Parents

DIRECTIONS TO MAKE THE BOOK: Copy the storybook for each student. Color and cut out along the dotted lines. Staple the eight pages together in numerical order.

BEFORE READING

1. Read the list of "**Tt**" words that appear in the story: **two, turtles, tons, top, TV, tired, tent, toy.**
2. Discuss the other words in the story: **play, at, in, they, have, of, with, watch, are, sleeping.**
3. Have the children look at the text and circle each uppercase **T** and lowercase **t**.

AFTER READING

1. Together read and discuss the story.
2. There are more pictures in the story that have the "**Tt**" sound. Can you find them? *(tumbling, telephone)*

MORE "Tt" ACTIVITIES

1. Sing, *I'm a Little Teapot*, and *Twinkle, Twinkle Little Star.*
2. Make a tambourine. Decorate two paper plates. Place the two plates together, put beans or rice on the inside, and tape together. Add streamers for extra fun.

5

They play with a toy lion.

7

Two tired turtles are sleeping in a tent.

2 — Cub played in the mud.

4 — Bug played in the mud.

1 — (Short Sound) Letter "Uu" Story

Suds in the Tub

3 — Duck played in the mud.

6

Cub, duck, and bug get in the tub.

8

Notes to Teachers/Parents

DIRECTIONS TO MAKE THE BOOK: Copy the storybook for each student. Color and cut out along the dotted lines. Staple the eight pages together in numerical order.

BEFORE READING ----------

1. Read the list of short **"Uu"** words that appear in the story: **suds, tub, cub, duck, bug, mud, rub.**

2. Discuss the other words in the story: **played, in, the, fill, with, and, get.**

3. Have the children look at the text and circle each lowercase **u.**

AFTER READING ----------

1. Together read and discuss the story.

2. There are more pictures in the story that have the short **"Uu"** sound. Can you find them? *(bubbles, umbrella)*

MORE SHORT "Uu" ACTIVITIES ----------

1. Bat a balloon "up" in the air.

2. How many new words can you make using these word families: –ub, –ud, –ut.

3. Fill a tub with water and have fun sinking and floating various objects.

5

Fill the tub with suds!

7

Rub, rub, rub!

2

Cute mule works.

4

He uses a tube of glue.

(Long Sound) Letter "Uu" Story

Cute Mule

1

3

He uses a ruler.

53

6

What did cute mule make?

8

Notes to Teachers/Parents

DIRECTIONS TO MAKE THE BOOK: Copy the storybook for each student. Color and cut out along the dotted lines. Staple the eight pages together in numerical order.

BEFORE READING

1. Read the list of long **"Uu"** words that appear in the story: **cute, mule, uses, ruler, tube, glue, blue, flute, music.**

2. Discuss the other words in the story: **works, he, a, of, pencil, what, did, make, to.**

3. Have the children look at the text and circle each lowercase **u.**

AFTER READING

1. Together read and discuss the story.

2. There are more pictures in the story that have the long **"Uu"** sound. Can you find them? *(unicorn, unicycle)*

MORE LONG "Uu" ACTIVITIES

1. On index cards, write the following words without the u: m_le, r_le, bl_e, fl_te, c_te, t_be, c_be. The children should add the "u" and read the words.

2. Draw a picture of a unicorn riding a unicycle.

5

He uses a blue pencil.

7

A flute to make music.

Letter "Vv" Story

A Very Special Day

2

It is a very special day.

4

She put violets in a vase.

3

Vanessa Vulture vacuumed.

He got his violin.

6

Notes to Teachers/Parents

DIRECTIONS TO MAKE THE BOOK: Copy the storybook for each student. Color and cut out along the dotted lines. Staple the eight pages together in numerical order.

BEFORE READING

1. Read the list of "**Vv**" words that appear in the story: **very, Vanessa, Vance, vulture, vacuumed, violets, vase, vest, violin, Valentine's.**

2. Discuss the other words in the story: **a, special, day, it, is, she, put, in, on, the, got, his, happy, he.**

3. Have the children look at the text and circle each uppercase **V** and lowercase **v**.

AFTER READING

1. Together read and discuss the story.

2. There are more pictures in the story that have the "**Vv**" sound. Can you find them? (van)

MORE "Vv" ACTIVITIES

1. Have a vegetable tasting party.

2. Make vegetable prints. Cut a variety of vegetables in half, dip in paint, and press onto paper.

3. Make a pennant with a large "**V**" for victory.

8

Vance Vulture put on a vest.

5

Happy Valentine's Day!

7

Letter "Ww" Story

Wendy
and the
Wagon

Wendy has a new wagon.

She put a worm in her wagon.

She put a walrus in her wagon.

6

She put a watermelon
in her wagon.

8

Notes to Teachers/Parents

DIRECTIONS TO MAKE THE BOOK: Copy the storybook for each student. Color and cut out along the dotted lines. Staple the eight pages together in numerical order.

BEFORE READING
1. Read the list of **"Ww"** words that appear in the story: **Wendy, wagon, worm, walrus, watch, watermelon, wow, what.**
2. Discuss the other words in the story: **and, a, new, she, put, in, her, full, the.**
3. Have the children look at the text and circle each uppercase **W** and lowercase **w**.

AFTER READING
1. Together read and discuss the story.
2. There are more pictures in the story that have the **"Ww"** sound. Can you find them? *(windmill, wind)*

MORE "Ww" ACTIVITIES
1. Sing, *I've Been Working on the Railroad.*
2. Glue wallpaper scraps on paper to make a collage.
3. Make wiggle worms. Use a straw that is wrapped in paper. Open one end of the straw and scrunch the paper down to the bottom of the straw. Remove the paper from the straw. Put a few drops of water on the paper and watch it wiggle.

5

She put a watch
in her wagon.

7

Wow! What a full wagon!

Page 2

Not many words begin with the letter "X."

Page 4

And "X" marks the spot.

Page 1

Letter "Xx" Story

The Sound of "X"

EXIT

Page 3

There is x-ray.

6

Box, fox, six, and mix all have "x" at the end.

8

Notes to Teachers/Parents

DIRECTIONS TO MAKE THE BOOK: Copy the storybook for each student. Color and cut out along the dotted lines. Staple the eight pages together in numerical order.

BEFORE READING ----------------------------------
1. Read the list of **"Xx"** words that appear in the story: **x-ray, exit, exam, fox, box, mix, six, xylophone.**
2. Discuss the other words in the story: **not, many, words, have, at, the, end, letter, there, is, and, can, hear, begin, with, marks, spot, all, you, in.**
3. Have the children look at the text and circle each uppercase **X** and lowercase **x**.

AFTER READING ----------------------------------
1. Together read and discuss the story.

MORE "Xx" ACTIVITIES ----------------------------------
1. Make a xylophone using 6 identical bottles or glasses. Fill each with different amounts of water. Hit lightly with a spoon and listen to the sounds.
2. Play tic-tac-toe using large and small **X**'s.

5

EXAM

Name _____

20 14 15 7
$+3$ $+2$ $+1$ $+8$
____   ____   ____   ____

12 7 13
-3 -4 -6
____   ____   ____

14
-6
____

$3 \times 5 =$ ____ $11 \times 2 =$ ____

In exam and exit you can hear the "x."

7

Can you hear the "x" in xylophone?

Letter "Yy" Story

Yummy, Yummy!

Yanni Yak is hungry.

He ate some yogurt.
Yummy, yummy!

He ate some yolks.
Yummy, yummy!

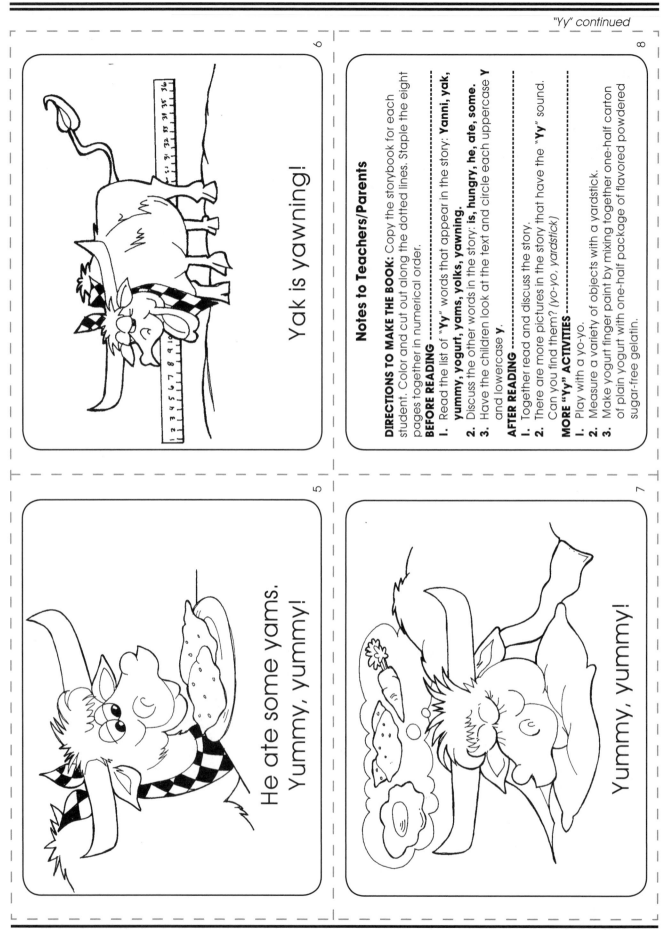

6

Yak is yawning!

8

Notes to Teachers/Parents

DIRECTIONS TO MAKE THE BOOK: Copy the storybook for each student. Color and cut out along the dotted lines. Staple the eight pages together in numerical order.

BEFORE READING
1. Read the list of "**Yy**" words that appear in the story: **Yanni, yak, yummy, yogurt, yams, yolks, yawning.**
2. Discuss the other words in the story: **is, hungry, he, ate, some.**
3. Have the children look at the text and circle each uppercase **Y** and lowercase **y**.

AFTER READING
1. Together read and discuss the story.
2. There are more pictures in the story that have the "**Yy**" sound. Can you find them? *(yo-yo, yardstick)*

MORE "Yy" ACTIVITIES
1. Play with a yo-yo.
2. Measure a variety of objects with a yardstick.
3. Make yogurt finger paint by mixing together one-half carton of plain yogurt with one-half package of flavored powdered sugar-free gelatin.

5

He ate some yams.
Yummy, yummy!

7

Yummy, yummy!

Letter "Zz" Story

Zoie's Zippy Toy

Zip, zap, zig, zag, zoom!

Zoie, what is that noise in your room?

Again, zip, zap, zig, zag, zoom!

6

Again,
zip, zap, zig, zag, zoom!

8

Notes to Teachers/Parents

DIRECTIONS TO MAKE THE BOOK: Copy the storybook for each student. Color and cut out along the dotted lines. Staple the eight pages together in numerical order.

BEFORE READING

1. Read the list of **"Zz"** words that appear in the story: **zip, zippy, zap, zag, zig, zoom, Zoie, Zoie-bot.**

2. Discuss the other words in the story: **what, is, that, noise, in, your, room, built, a, to, clean, my, again.**

3. Have the children look at the text and circle each uppercase **Z** and lowercase **z.**

AFTER READING

1. Together read and discuss the story.

MORE "Zz" ACTIVITIES

1. Sing, *Zip-a-dee Doo-dah,* and *We're Going to the Zoo.*
2. Make a set of animal cards and play zoo memory match.
3. Make a zigzag hopscotch.
4. Read, *On Beyond Zebra,* by Dr. Seuss.

5

Zoie, what is that
noise in your room?

7

I built a Zoie-bot
to clean my room.